CUTTING EDGE MEDICINE

Fighting Infectious Diseases

Carol Ballard

WORLD ALMANAC® LIBRARY

Please visit our Web site at: **www.garethstevens.com**
For a free color catalog describing World Almanac® Library's list of high-quality books
and multimedia programs, call 1-800-848-2928 (USA) or 1-800-387-3178 (Canada).
World Almanac® Library's fax: (414) 332-3567.

Library of Congress Cataloging-in-Publication Data available upon request from publisher.
Fax (414) 336-0157 for the attention of the Publishing Records Department.

ISBN 978-0-8368-7864-6 (lib. bdg.)

This North American edition first published in 2007 by
World Almanac® Library
A Member of the WRC Media Family of Companies
330 West Olive Street, Suite 100
Milwaukee, WI 53212 USA

This U.S. edition copyright © 2007 by World Almanac® Library.
Original edition copyright © 2007 by Arcturus Publishing Limited.

Produced by Arcturus Publishing Limited.
Editor: Alex Woolf
Designer: Nick Phipps
Consultant: Dr. Eleanor Clarke

World Almanac® Library editor: Carol Ryback
World Almanac® Library designer: Kami M. Strunsee
World Almanac® Library art direction: Tammy West
World Almanac® Library production: Jessica Yanke and Robert Kraus

The right of Andrew Solway to be identified as the author of this work has been
asserted by him in accordance with the Copyright, Designs and Patents Act, 1988.

Photo credits: Science Photo Library: / BSIP/Laurent/FILIN 5; / Astrid and Hanns-Frieder Michler 6; / Sheila Terry 8,
10; / Volker Steger, Peter Arnold, Inc. 13; / CNRI 14; / D. Phillips 17; / NIBSC 19, 21; / Steve Gschmeissner 23; /
Andrew Syred 25; / Sinclair Stammers 27; / Juergen Berger28; / Stem Jems 30; / John Walsh 33, 35; / Bob Gibbons
37; / Saturn Stills, cover and 38; / AJ Photo/Hop Americain 41; / TH Photo-Werbung 43; / Geoff Tompkinson 45, 47;
/ James King-Holmes 48; / AJ Photo 50; / Dr. Kari Lounatmaa 53; / Philippepsaila 54; / NASA 57; / Pascal Goetgheluck 59.

Printed in China

1 2 3 4 5 6 7 8 9 10 10 09 08 07 06

Contents

YA
616.9
B212

CHAPTER 1

What Are Infectious Diseases?

An infectious disease is an illness that passes from one person to another. For example, if one person in a family has a bad cold, it often spreads to other family members. A common cold is therefore an infectious disease. Other examples include chickenpox, influenza (often called flu), and measles. Illnesses such as asthma, arthritis, and heart disease do not spread from one person to another, so they are not infectious diseases.

Almost everybody in the world is affected by an infectious disease at some time during their lives. Some infectious diseases are mild, some are serious, and others are life-threatening. For example, a cold makes you uncomfortable for just a few days, but measles can make you feel very ill and may have long-term effects —and typhoid can rapidly kill large numbers of people.

CUTTING EDGE MOMENTS

The beginning of epidemiology

One of the first people to study the spread of infectious diseases was John Snow, who lived in London, England, in the nineteenth century. Snow was appalled by the squalid living conditions of many people and was convinced that the lack of clean water contributed to the number of infections they suffered. In 1854, he studied how an infection spread during a cholera outbreak in London. Snow traced its source to a contaminated water pump. By removing the pump handle, he stopped the contaminated water from being used, and this stopped the infection from spreading any further. Snow's method of studying outbreaks of infection gave rise to the science we now call epidemiology. Modern scientists who study the occurrence, frequency, and spread of infectious diseases are called epidemiologists.

This woman has a cold, which is an infectious disease.

Killer diseases

Millions of people around the world die each year from infectious diseases. We know this because information about the health of the population in each country is collected by the World Health Organization (WHO). This information is combined to give a global picture. Some of the information collected tells us the total number of people who die each year from different diseases. In 2002, the total world population was 6.2 billion, and a total of 57 million people died. Out of these, about a quarter of all deaths were due to infectious diseases. The biggest killers were HIV/AIDS and pneumonia. Next came diarrheal diseases such as cholera and typhoid, followed by tuberculosis (TB) and malaria. There are many possible causes of infectious disease. Cramped living conditions, poverty, lack of a sanitary water supply, poor nutrition, economic class, famine, and drought all play a hand in diseases that rage out of control—especially in developing countries.

Infectious diseases and the human body

Understanding how the human body is organized helps us understand how infectious diseases affect the body and how the body responds to them. The human body, like all other living organisms, consists of millions of tiny units called cells. A cell is the smallest complete unit of a living organism. Cells that have a similar structure and function are grouped together to make tissues. Tissues are grouped together into organs, such as the lungs, which carry out a single function.

Organs that carry out similar or connected functions are grouped together to make systems. For example, muscle cells are grouped together to make muscle tissue. Together, muscle tissues and nerve tissue make an organ, the heart. The heart, blood vessels, and

Someone who eats improperly stored or unsanitary food could develop an infection.

CUTTING EDGE   SCIENCE

How do infectious diseases pass from person to person?

This table shows some of the ways by which an infectious disease can spread:

how infection is spread	example	diseases spread in this way
direct contact	a) touch b) mixing body fluids such as saliva or blood	impetigo (a skin infection) HIV/AIDS
airborne	germs released into the air by coughs and sneezes	influenza, colds
food	inadequate storage or cooking	salmonella (a type of food poisoning)
water	germs from poor sanitation and lack of clean water	cholera, typhoid
insects	insects spread an infection by biting or laying eggs	malaria

blood make up the circulatory system, which maintains the circulation of blood around the body.

Just about every part of the body can suffer from an infection. Some infectious diseases affect a single organ, while others may affect several organs or an entire body system. In some infections, the effects are due simply to the infection itself. Some other infections produce toxins (poisonous chemicals) that can have serious effects. Other infections do little damage themselves, but the body's reaction to the infection causes serious effects.

Common or rare

Some infectious diseases, such as a cold or sore throat, are common. Many people suffer from them sometimes several times a year. Others, such as tetanus and rabies, are rare in developed countries, and we may not hear of anyone suffering from them. Some infectious diseases occur in all seasons, while others are more common in one season than another. For example, more people usually suffer from influenza in the winter than in the summer.

The infectious diseases that are common vary from one part of the world to another. For example, many people who live in countries close to the equator suffer from malaria (an infectious disease caused by a parasite transmitted in the bite of infected mosquitoes), but malaria is uncommon in cooler countries. Infectious diseases that occur naturally in a country are considered endemic. At any particular time, a small proportion of the population of a country might be expected to suffer from an endemic infection.

During the 1918 influenza pandemic, many people, like these soldiers in Seattle, Washington, wore masks to try to avoid infection. Unfortunately, the masks were not very effective in preventing the spread of disease.

Epidemics and pandemics

An infection that spreads rapidly throughout a population is called an epidemic. This occurs when an outbreak of an infectious disease hits a particular town or area. For example, a single case of chickenpox often spreads quickly within a school and results in other children becoming infected. Friends and relatives can spread the chickenpox virus to other schools and other nearby towns.

If an epidemic spreads over a wider area, either within one country or from one country to other countries, eventually affecting a very large number of people, it is called a pandemic. For example, in 1916 a pandemic of poliomylelitis spread across twenty U.S. states and infected nearly 30,000 people, of whom about 7,000 died. The possibility of a pandemic worried many people in 2002, when a few isolated cases of severe acute respiratory syndrome (SARS) in China were rapidly followed by more cases around the world. SARS spreads through coughs and sneezes. Fortunately, although cases were widespread, the numbers infected remained small, and the outbreak did not have serious consequences.

The Black Death

Throughout history, epidemics and pandemics have killed many millions of people. One disease that was particularly feared was bubonic plague. Victims developed large, black swellings in the armpits and groin. It could kill within a few days. During the fourteenth century, a bubonic plague pandemic, which became known as the Black Death, swept across Asia, North Africa, and Europe. In some places, the plague wiped out at least one-quarter of the population. Less severe epidemics of plague have also occurred—for example, an outbreak of plague occurred in London, England, in 1665. The Great Fire of London that raged through the city the following year halted the spread of the plague.

CUTTING EDGE MOMENTS

1918 influenza pandemic

In the spring of 1918, during the final year of World War I (WWI), a killer disease spread around the world: Influenza. The outbreak began in the central United States, where it affected about 25 percent of the population. U.S. soldiers bound for the war probably carried that virus strain to Europe, where it spread rapidly across the globe. Hospitals throughout Europe were overwhelmed by the pandemic. (It was called the Spanish Flu because Spain's newspapers publicized the outbreak, while countries involved in fighting WWI did not.) To cope with the huge numbers of sick people, many countries set up extra hospital wards in schools and other buildings. No known treatment existed. Many people also died from secondary bacterial infections that followed the flu infection. By the time the pandemic subsided in 1919, at least twenty million people around the world had died of influenza—more than had been killed during WWI.

This woodcut, from a book published in 1493, shows Christopher Columbus landing on Hispaniola (the island that now holds Haiti and the Dominican Republic).

Resistance to disease

After exposure to an infection, the body is often able to resist a future attack by the same infection. For example, someone who gets mumps in childhood is unlikely to suffer from mumps a second time—he or she has built up a resistance to mumps (*see page 31 for an explanation of how people develop resistance to diseases*).

If a high proportion of a population is exposed to a disease-causing agent and then develops a resistance to that infection, a subsequent outbreak of that infection will be less serious should it occur. Only the young, who have not previously been exposed to the infection, and the sick and elderly, who are less able to withstand infections, will succumb to (suffer from) the disease.

Hundreds of years ago, people from one continent had little or no contact with people from other continents. They were only exposed to the infectious diseases that were common in their own lands. When Europeans and others began exploring the world, they carried along their own particular endemic infectious diseases. This had serious—and sometimes disastrous—consequences for the native peoples in the countries to which the Europeans or other explorers traveled. The native peoples had no resistance to new diseases, which were completely new to their immune systems. Many natives died as a result of infections such as chickenpox and measles, which were not considered serious by the explorers.

CUTTING EDGE   FACTS

Sixteenth-century explorers and infectious disease in the Americas

The first contact between Europeans and the peoples of North and South America occurred in the last decade of the fifteenth century. At that time, Christopher Columbus and other explorers began to sail across the Atlantic Ocean, landing in and around the Caribbean. They brought with them many infectious diseases, including smallpox, chickenpox, measles, typhoid, cholera, scarlet fever, and influenza. These diseases were unknown in the Western Hemisphere, so the native peoples had no resistance to them. An epidemic that may have been swine fever—an infection usually associated with pigs—swept through the island of Hispaniola in 1493. Serious outbreaks of other infectious diseases followed. Smallpox devastated the native population of Mexico, which fell to one-tenth its previous level within fifty years of the arrival of the Europeans.

Explorers took the infections with them as they ventured deeper into the Americas. In North America in 1763, British Army officers ordered that blankets that had been exposed to smallpox be given to the Native Americans in order to infect them with the disease. No one knows the exact number of native peoples who died from European infections, but some historians estimate that it may have been as many as 90 percent of the population (nine out of ten people died). The Europeans used the infections to their advantage and had a much easier time conquering and claiming new lands for their kings.

Discovering how diseases spread

People have known that diseases could spread from one person to another for centuries, but it was only during the nineteenth century that scientists began to understand how and why this happened. The work of several scientists, including Robert Koch and Louis Pasteur, proved that infectious diseases were caused by tiny living things called microorganisms. This idea was called the germ theory. Microorganisms, or microbes, were too small to be seen with the eye and could only be studied using microscopes. Slowly, scientists developed techniques for growing the microbes in the laboratory and studying their life cycles. Scientists began to search for chemicals that could kill microbes and thus cure infections. Other

CUTTING EDGE   MOMENTS

When were microbes first seen?

Anton van Leeuwenhoek (1632–1723), who lived in Delft, in the Netherlands, was a keen amateur scientist. A textile merchant by trade, he used magnifying lenses to help him inspect the quality of cloth. Using hand-ground lenses, he designed and built several microscopes. He examined drops of rainwater, pond water, and well water—as well as scrapings from his teeth—with one of his microscopes, and was very surprised to see tiny living organisms moving around. He thought they looked like tiny animals, and so he called them "animalcules." Van Leeuwenhoek drew what he saw and sent his drawings to the Royal Society of England in a letter. They were published in the journal of the Royal Society in 1677. This was the first recorded observation of bacteria. It would be almost two hundred years before scientists proved that these bacteria were the cause of some infectious diseases.

scientists searched for ways of preventing a person from developing an infection. Many of the medicines that are standard treatments for infectious diseases today evolved from this research.

Following the pioneering work by John Snow in the nineteenth century (*see sidebar, page 4*), the link between dirty water and some infectious diseases slowly became established and accepted.

Today, the lack of a clean water supply and adequate sanitation still contributes to the spread of infectious diseases such as cholera and typhoid. Although cholera poses an insignificant risk in developed countries, it leads to health problems in many developing countries. Keeping ourselves, our possessions, and our surroundings clean and hygienic helps prevent infections. Hygienic preparation and storage of food is also important in the control of infections like those that cause food poisoning. For example, properly storing foods such as meat and milk in a refrigerator rather than at room temperature helps keep them fresher longer.

Anton van Leeuwenhoek used this primitive microscope to observe bacteria more than three hundred years ago. Magnifications of up to two hundred times were possible. He placed the specimen on the tip of the needle, which in this image lines up with the lens. Two screws helped adjust the position of the specimen. This device measures only 3 to 4 inches (7.62 to 10.16 centimeters). It was held up to a light for use.

CHAPTER 2

Pathogens and Infectious Diseases

Anything that causes an infectious disease is called a pathogen. Many pathogens are microorganisms, but some pathogens are larger organisms. Pathogens can be divided into four main groups: bacteria, viruses, fungi, and other parasites. When a pathogen enters the body, it triggers a reaction by the body's immune system (*see sidebar, page 31*). In many cases, the immune system detects and destroys the pathogen before it causes any harm. In some cases, though, the pathogen multiplies very quickly and causes problems before the immune system can stage an effective reaction.

Bacteria

There are probably more bacteria on Earth than any other type of organism. We have bacteria living on our skin, in our intestines, and on every surface around us. Some bacteria are good for us, such as those that live in the intestines and help us digest our food. Other bacteria, however, cause a wide range of infectious diseases.

Bacteria are single-celled organisms. Some are rod-shaped, some are spherical, and some are spiral. Some move by waving their flagellum, a tiny, hair-like structure, back and forth. Although many different types of bacteria exist, they share some basic

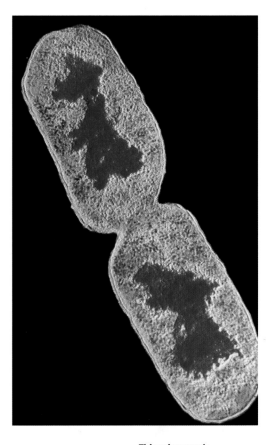

This micrograph (a photo taken through any kind of microscope) shows two cells of *Escherichia coli*, a rod-shaped bacterium that can cause digestive system infections.

similarities. Most are less than 0.001 mm long. They have a complex outer layer, or cell wall, made from a mixture of proteins, sugars, and fats. Inside, the jelly-like cytoplasm often contains granules that provide food for the bacterium.

Bacterial cells differ in important ways from animal cells. Animal cells contain their genetic information in material called chromatin within the nucleus. During cell division, the chromatin forms threadlike structures called chromosomes. These structures carry the genetic information from one generation to the next. Bacterial cells do not have a nucleus. Instead, the chromosome is just curled up in the cytoplasm. Some bacteria also contain one or more much smaller, circular strands of genetic material, called plasmids.

Most bacteria feed by releasing digestive enzymes. These are proteins that break down food outside the bacterium. The bacteria absorbs the nutrients that are released. Each bacterium produces and releases poisonous waste by-products, called toxins. In many bacterial infections, the toxins rather than the bacteria themselves, make people sick.

CUTTING EDGE   SCIENCE

Multiplying bacteria
This diagram makes it is easier to understand what happens when a single bacterium divides.

1
2
4
8
16

Bacteria are so tiny that more than 250,000 of them can fit on the head of a pin. Under ideal temperature and moisture conditions, a bacterium doubles itself every 20 minutes—or three times an hour. Over the course of 12 divisions, one bacterium would multiply as follows: 1; 2; 4; 8; 16; 32; 64; 128; 256; 512; 1,024; 2,048; 4,096. It takes only 12 divisions, or four hours, for one bacterium to become 4,096 bacteria! Just think how many bacteria would exist after 12, 24, or 48 hours!

Bacteria have a very simple life cycle. A bacterium grows bigger until it is too big to exist as one cell. It then splits into two to make two new bacteria. This division process is called fission. Each of the new bacteria cells grows and then divides into two, and each of these in turn grows and divides into two, and so on. The group of bacteria that develops is known as a colony.

There are many different types of bacteria that cause a variety of infections. Bacteria are responsible for abscesses and boils (infected pores in the skin), sore throats, food poisoning, and septic (dirty and infected) wounds, as well as life-threatening diseases. Some of the most common infectious diseases caused by bacteria include the following:

Tuberculosis (TB) is caused by the bacterium *Mycobacterium tuberculosis*. It affects nearly one-third of the world's population. In developed countries, the usual site of infection is the lungs, while in parts of Africa, abdominal tuberculosis is also common. Other body areas may also be affected. As the bacteria multiply, they damage small sections of lung tissue. At this stage, the infection is still treatable. If the infection spreads throughout the lungs, it leads to breathing difficulties, and—if untreated—eventual death.

CUTTING EDGE   SCIENCE

Naming bacteria
Bacteria are grouped according to their shape. Each group has a special name.

name	shape	example of illness or condition caused by each type of bacteria
Coccus	spherical a) in chains—*Streptococcus* b) in clusters—*Staphylococcus* c) in pairs—*Gonococci*	scarlet fever abscesses pneumonia
Bacillus	rod-shaped	typhoid
Vibrio	bent rod-shaped	cholera
Spirilla (or Spirochaetes)	spiral	syphilis

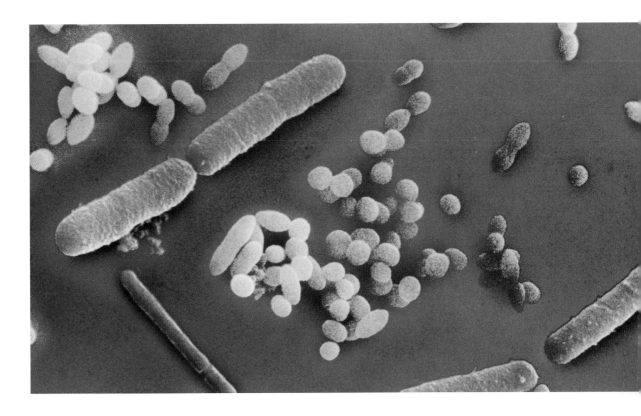

Typhoid occurs when the bacterium *Salmonella typhi* infects the intestines. Bacteria leave the body in the feces. In places where clean water is unavailable and sanitation is poor, food and water may become contaminated by feces, spreading the infection to other people. At first, typhoid causes flu-like symptoms, followed by abdominal pain and diarrhea. Without treatment, dehydration (too little water in the body) can become severe and the infection may be fatal.

The human gut contains rod-shaped and spherical bacteria, such as these. Rod-shaped bacteria are bacilli. Ball-shaped bacteria are cocci.

Cholera is an intestinal infection caused by the bacterium *Vibrio cholerae*. It leads to vomiting and diarrhea, which in turn lead to severe dehydration and death. Cholera spreads via feces and contaminated water and is therefore a particular problem in areas without adequate sanitation and clean water supplies.

Tetanus is caused by the bacterium *Clostridium tetani* that is found naturally in soil. The bacteria enter the body via a wound in the skin. As *Clostridium tetani* multiply, they produce a toxin that first paralyzes the jaw muscles and then other muscles.

Bacterial meningitis occurs when the fluid that surrounds the brain and spinal cord is infected with the *Meningococcus* bacterium. The infection irritates the meninges (membranes surrounding the brain), and they become swollen. Meningitis spreads from one person to another via coughs and sneezes. It may begin very suddenly with headache, sore neck, and fever, or it may develop more slowly over several days. As the bacteria multiply, they can infect the blood and spread throughout the body, causing a skin rash. Bacterial meningitis is rare in most developed countries, but is a major killer in some parts of the world, especially in West Africa.

Viruses

Most viruses are many times smaller than bacteria. Viruses have a wide variety of shapes and structures, but they all have a protein coat, called a capsule, enclosing a central core of genetic material. Viruses are not complete cells. They have no nucleus, cytoplasm, or cell membrane. They do not carry out basic life processes such as growing, feeding, respiration, or getting rid of waste products, and they are unable to reproduce without a host cell. For these reasons, they are considered particles instead of actual cells.

Viruses can survive on their own, but they must be inside a living cell (a host cell) in order to reproduce. In most cases, the virus particle sticks to the host's cell membrane. Either the virus's

CUTTING EDGE MOMENTS

The first electron microscopes

In the 1930s, more advanced microscopes enabled scientists to study viruses for the first time. All of the earlier microscopes worked by shining a beam of light onto or through the object that scientists wanted to study. The maximum magnification achieved using a light microscope was about 2,000x (2,000 times)—not enough to reveal details of structures inside cells.

In 1932, two German scientists, Max Knoll and Ernest Ruska, developed a new type of microscope, a transmission electron microscope (TEM). Instead of using a beam of light, the TEM shone a beam of electrons (focused by magnets) through the material being studied. Although the first instrument only magnified a specimen by 17x, the technology was refined and developed rapidly, eventually providing sufficient magnification to allow scientists to see inside cells in great detail—and to see the structure of viruses for the first time.

In 1952, Sir Charles Oatley, an English scientist, developed a scanning electron microscope (SEM). This shone a beam of electrons at the surface of an object to produce a three-dimensional image. Present-day electron microscopes can magnify objects more than two million times!

genetic material or the complete virus particle then enters the host cell. Once inside the host cell, the virus's genetic material hijacks the cell's mechanisms. It stops the original (host) cell from carrying out its normal processes and instead makes the host produce lots of copies of the virus's genetic material and capsules. These escape from the original host cell and infect other host cells—and the whole process begins again. The host cells are destroyed by the virus particles, and it is this destruction that leads to the symptoms of the disease caused by each virus.

This micrograph shows a vaccinia virus particle (pink) inside a human cell (yellow). The vaccinia virus is very similar to the virus that causes cowpox, a disease of cattle and humans.

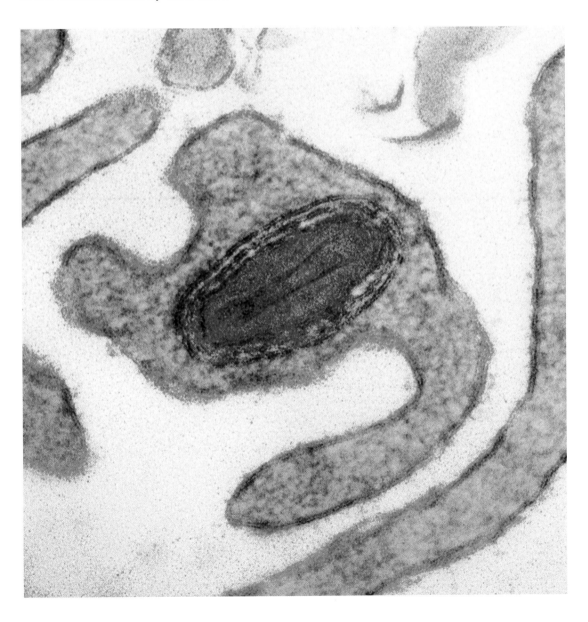

Like bacteria, many different types of viruses cause a multitude of infections. Viruses are responsible for colds and flu, warts, and childhood diseases, such as chickenpox, measles, and mumps—as well as life-threatening diseases that affect people of all ages. Two viral infections that have received much publicity in recent years are HIV/AIDS and SARS.

HIV/AIDS The first recorded case of HIV/AIDS occurred in 1981. It is caused by the Human Immunodeficiency Virus (HIV), which attacks the body's immune system. A person who is infected with HIV is said to be HIV positive. Eventually, HIV weakens the immune system so much that the person becomes ill with other infections. At that stage, the person with HIV is said to have developed AIDS (Acquired Immune Deficiency Syndrome). HIV/AIDS is spread during sexual intercourse from an infected person to a non-infected person. Many governments advise people to use a condom to reduce the risk of becoming infected. HIV/AIDS can also be spread by contact with infected blood—for example, among drug users who share needles. HIV/AIDS is a serious global pandemic: In 2005, about 3.1 million people died from AIDS. Scientists predict that by 2010, about 85 million people worldwide will be HIV positive.

CUTTING EDGE SCIENTISTS

David Ho, virologist

David Ho was born on November 3, 1952 in Taiwan. His family moved to the United States and settled in Los Angeles, California. Because Ho spoke no English, he found school very difficult at first, but he quickly learned the language. Ho studied physics at the Massachusetts Institute of Technology and the California Institute of Technology, but switched to molecular biology and won a scholarship to Harvard Medical School. There, he saw some of the first cases of AIDS and decided to focus on it. Ho began to search for ways of combating the infection at its earliest stages. He devised the "cocktails" (mixtures) of antiviral drugs that are now widely used in the treatment of AIDS. In his current research, Ho continues to look for improved treatments and for an AIDS vaccine. David Ho was appointed Director of the Aaron Diamond AIDS Research Center in New York City in 1991, and in 1996 was named *Time* magazine's Man of the Year.

SARS stands for Severe Acute Respiratory Syndrome and is caused by a virus similar to the virus responsible for the common cold. The virus infects the lungs, where it causes severe damage. It spreads rapidly through coughs and sneezes from an infected person to others in close contact. Worldwide panic followed a SARS outbreak in 2002. International travel carried the virus around the world. In many countries, anyone showing SARS-like symptoms and any people who had been in physical contact with them were quarantined (kept away from others) until the outbreak was brought under control.

A lymphocyte—a type of white blood cell—appears green in this micrograph. It is infected with particles of HIV virus (red).

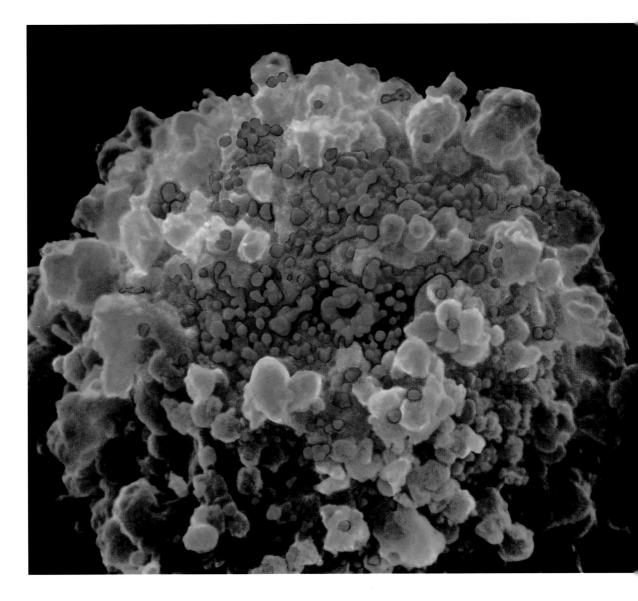

Fungi

Fungi consist of long threads called hyphae (singular: hypha). These have a structure similar to regular cells, including an outer wall and cytoplasm with a space, or vacuole, at the center. Unlike other cells, they contain multiple nuclei spread throughout the cytoplasm. The hyphae form a network called a mycelium that spreads throughout the material on which the hyphae grow. Fungi absorb food from the material they are growing on. Most reproduce by releasing tiny cells called spores from special hyphae called fruiting bodies. The spores then germinate (begin to grow) to form a new mycelium.

Some fungi cause infectious diseases in plants, while others affect animals. There are more than seventy-five thousand known species of fungi, but only about two hundred cause infections in humans. Most fungal infections affect the skin rather than internal organs, and many fungal infections affect people whose bodies are already weakened from another illness or some other factor.

CUTTING EDGE — FACTS

Useful fungi

Not all fungi are bad news! Some, such as yeast, are useful. We use yeasts to make bread. Yeasts are also used to ferment sugar to make wine and beer. Other fungi turn milk into yogurt. The mushrooms that we eat are also fungi. The first antibiotic chemicals were extracted from fungi, and many antibiotics today are still derived from them.

Thrush is a common human fungal infection caused by the fungus *Candida albicans*. It usually affects the mouth or vagina, although it can also affect other body parts. In the mouth, white patches appear on the gums, lips, and inside of the cheeks. A vaginal infection of thrush causes a white discharge. *Candida albicans* is present in a healthy digestive system and does not normally cause any problems. Thrush can flare up elsewhere in the body for several reasons, including pregnancy, diabetes, use of oral contraceptives, use of antibiotics, or wearing tight nylon clothing.

Athlete's foot and ringworm are other common fungal infections that have different names depending on which part of the body is affected. In athlete's foot, the mycelium of the fungus *Trichophyton* grows on the skin between the toes and spreads easily to another person via contaminated towels, floors, and clothing. Athlete's foot is common among people with sweaty feet and among those who do not dry their feet thoroughly after bathing or swimming. It often spreads via shower rooms and floors in health clubs.

Ringworm is caused by a similar fungus, *Microsporum*, on the scalp. Ringworm gets its name from the circular rings that appear on the scalp. As the fungus grows outward, it dies at the center, creating a red itchy ring that gradually increases in size. Another fungus, *Epidermophyton*, causes ringworm in the groin area. Each of these fungi grow best in warm, damp conditions. They usually spread by direct contact with an infected person.

A micrograph of a human nail infected with athlete's foot. The red structures are spores from the fungus *Tricophyton*.

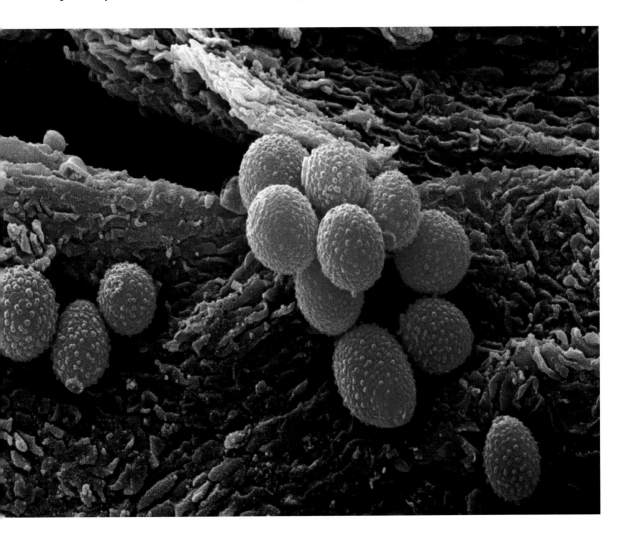

Parasites

Organisms that live off another living organism and damage it are called parasites. Humans and other animals can be infected by a wide range of parasites, both common and rare. Different parasites thrive in different conditions, so certain species are found in specific locations around the world, depending on the climate.

Some parasites are single-celled organisms called protozoa. They have a cell membrane, cytoplasm, and a nucleus. Some have long hair-like structures called flagellae that help them move around. Protozoa multiply by dividing, like bacteria, or by "budding," which is a type of cloning process in which small outgrowths of the cell swell and break off to form new cells. Protozoa can survive cold and dry conditions outside a host by forming cysts—structures that lie dormant (inactive)—but which develop into new protozoan cells when they reenter a host.

Some parasites are larger, multi-celled organisms. Fleas and lice, for example, are parasites that live on the surface of the body and feed on the host's blood. Other parasites, such as liver flukes (flatworms that infest the liver), live inside the host's body and feed directly on the host's blood or body tissues.

CUTTING EDGE   FACTS

Discovering words

Knowing the origins of words can help us to understand their meaning or give us extra information:

pathogen comes from two Greek words:
pathos—suffering
genes—to give rise to
Most pathogens cause suffering.

parasite comes from two Greek words:
para—beside
sitos—food
So, parasites live "beside their food"—or even in it!

protozoa comes from two Greek words:
proto—first
zoa—animal
Protozoans are thought to be among the very first animals that developed on Earth.

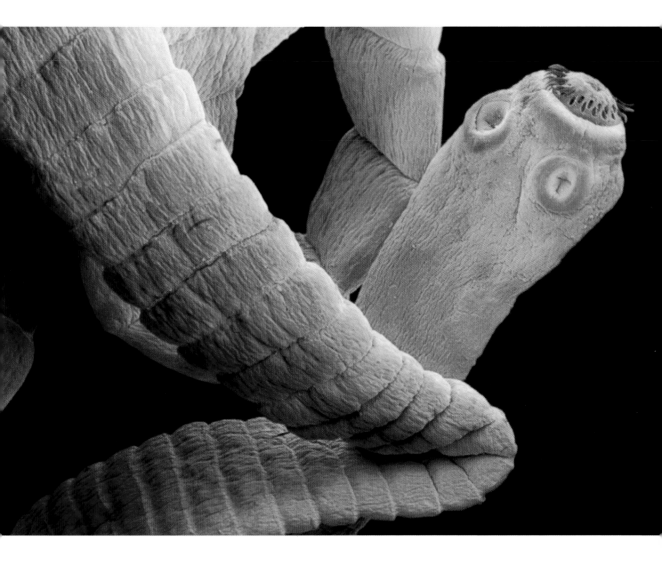

Parasitic infections can spread easily from person to person. Many parasites produce eggs that leave the body in the feces. If hygiene and sanitation is poor—for example, if drinking water becomes contaminated by human waste—the eggs can get into other people. The eggs mature into adult parasites, which produce more eggs, and so the cycle continues. Some parasites, such as those responsible for malaria and sleeping sickness, rely on insects to spread them to a new host.

Insects that carry and transmit diseases are called vectors. Some parasites, such as tapeworms, spend part of their life cycle living in other animals such as cows or pigs. The eggs of these parasites are transferred to people when people eat the meat of an infected animal. In that case, the meat is the vector for the parasite's eggs.

A micrograph of a tapeworm shows the head with suckers and hooklets that it uses to anchor itself to the inside of the host's intestines.

25

Parasites are responsible for many different infectious diseases. These include the following:

Malaria is caused by the protozoa *Plasmodium* and spreads via an insect vector. When a mosquito bites and sucks the blood of an infected person, the insect picks up the protozoa. The infection is then passed to the next person the mosquito bites. Most cases of malaria occur in tropical areas of the world. Malaria causes fever and vomiting and, if not treated, may result in kidney and liver damage and eventually death.

CUTTING EDGE   SCIENCE

Malaria and sickle cell anemia

Sickle cell anemia is an illness that is common in the same areas of the world as malaria. It causes red blood cells (RBCs) to become distorted and carry oxygen around the body less efficiently than in healthy people. It is an inherited condition that is passed from one generation to the next. To develop the full condition, an individual must inherit two copies of the sickle cell gene, one from each parent. People who inherit a sickle cell gene from one parent and a normal gene from the other develop a milder condition called sickle cell trait. Scientists have discovered that people with sickle cell trait are less likely to suffer from malaria than other people. This is because the malaria parasite, which spends part of its life cycle living in RBCs, cannot survive in sickled RBCs, because they rupture and prevent the parasite from reproducing. Also, the protein in RBCs that transports oxygen around the body (hemoglobin) is different in sickled cells, and the malaria parasite cannot digest it. It is therefore difficult for the malaria parasite to survive in people with sickle cell trait. In this way, sickle cell trait offers some protection against malaria.

Sleeping sickness occurs mainly in Africa. It is caused by the protozoa *Trypanosoma*, which infects the blood and brain and damages the nervous system. The infection is spread from person to person via an insect vector, the tsetse fly.

Schistosomiasis also known as bilharzia, is caused by a parasitic flatworm, *Schistosoma*. It occurs mainly in tropical areas. The infection is spread in the form of eggs via feces or urine from

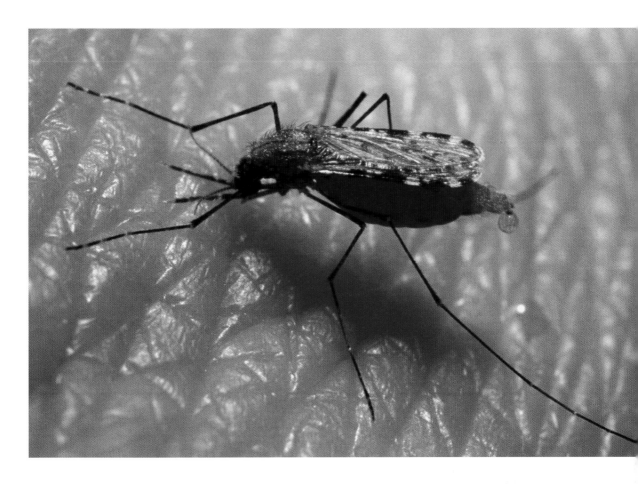

infected people. The eggs then develop inside freshwater snails and are released as larvae. The larvae penetrate the skin of people who bathe in the infected water. Once inside the body, the larvae infect blood vessels in the intestine. Schistomosiasis causes diarrhea and liver damage. If not treated, it may be fatal.

Tapeworms spread via eggs in feces from an infected animal or person. There are several different types of tapeworm, but the most common is the beef tapeworm, *Taenia saginata*. When the eggs are eaten by another animal, such as a cow, they hatch into larvae and infect the muscles. The larvae can spread to people who eat the meat of the animal. The tapeworm attaches itself to the intestine and absorbs nutrients from food passing through the digestive system. The person may lose weight and become weak due to lack of nutrients. Cooking meat thoroughly kills the tapeworm larvae and prevents its spread.

A mosquito bites human skin to feed on blood. The protozoa that cause malaria are passed on via the mosquito's saliva.

How do pathogens get into the body?

There are millions of microorganisms and other pathogens around us! Very few of the items that we handle every day will be completely free from pathogens. The skin serves as the body's first line of defense against them. This waterproof outer layer acts as a barrier that pathogens such as bacteria and viruses cannot penetrate. If the skin is damaged—for example, from a cut—dirt and microorganisms may enter the body via the damaged area. They may cause a localized infection (an infection that affects a small part of the body) or, if the microorganisms enter the bloodstream, they may cause a widespread infection often called blood poisoning or septicemia.

Another entry route for pathogens is via our food and drink. If foods are not properly stored, prepared, or cooked, they may contain pathogens that we take into our bodies when we eat. Some,

A cluster of *Staphylococcus* bacteria (yellow) sits among the tiny hairs (blue) that line the human airways. This type of bacteria causes diseases ranging from minor skin infections to serious illnesses such as pneumonia.

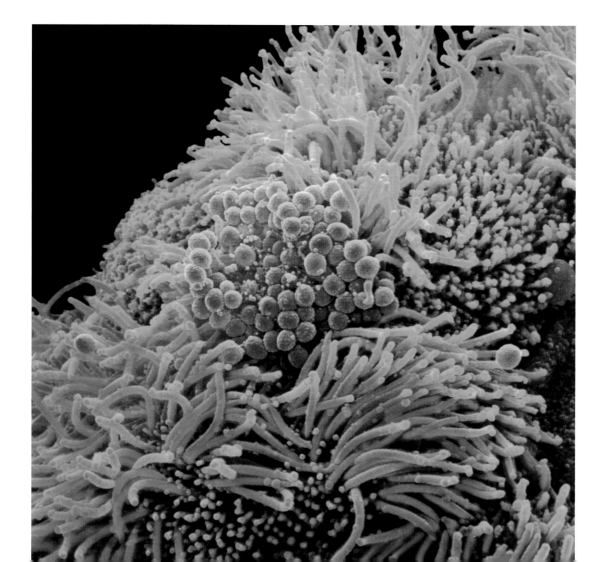

such as the bacterium *Listeria salmonella*, multiply in the food and continue to multiply in the digestive system. Others, such as the bacterium *Clostridium botulinum*, produce toxins that accumulate in the food. Both the microorganisms and the toxins cause an illness known as food poisoning. The symptoms are abdominal pain, diarrhea, and vomiting.

A third entry route for pathogens is via the airways. Microorganisms in the air enter the airways and travel to the lungs when we breathe. Tiny hairs line the nasal cavity and the airways, trapping some dirt and microbes. Some microorganisms evade this defense. When they reach a part of the body that provides the conditions which they need to live, they multiply. This can cause localized infections such as tonsillitis, or "strep throat." Microorganisms can also cause more serious infections, such as bronchitis, pneumonia, and tuberculosis.

Some microorganisms are passed from one person to another via medical processes such as blood transfusions. Today, extensive testing on all blood products helps ensure that infections will not be passed on by such procedures.

Some microorganisms, such as the HIV virus, are very fragile and can only survive outside a host for a minute or two. Others are more robust and can survive outside a host for longer periods. For example, *Escherichia coli*, a bacterium that causes food poisoning, can survive for up to twenty-four hours outside a host. Some microorganisms can survive outside a host, often as spores (a dormant stage in the microorganism's life cycle), for many years.

CUTTING EDGE   FACTS

Anthrax survival

Anthrax is a fatal lung disease of livestock, such as sheep and cows, that can also infect humans. During World War II, the British government explored the use of anthrax as a biological weapon. They exploded a bomb filled with anthrax spores on the Scottish island of Gruinard. Within a few days, the sheep on the island began dying. Anthrax spores can survive in soil, so the island was quarantined for nearly half a century. In 1990, forty-eight years after the release of the anthrax spores, the British government declared Gruinard Island anthrax-free, and the quarantine lifted.

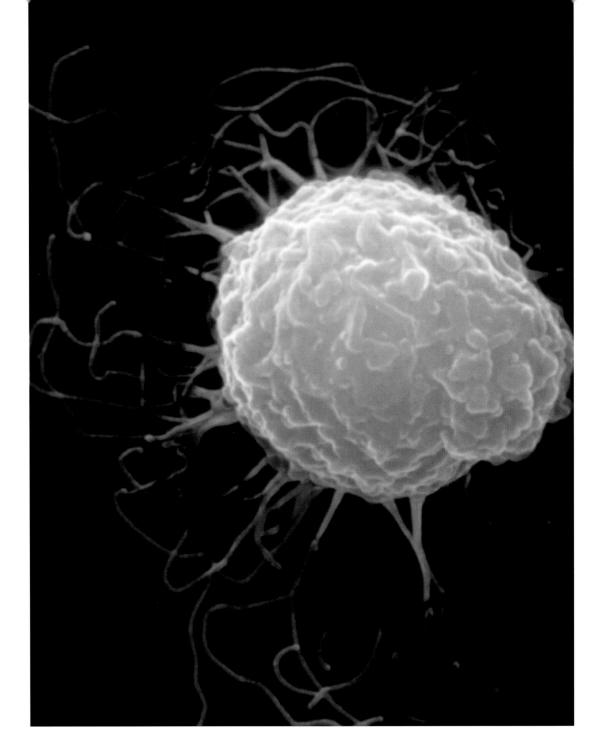

How does the body react to microorganisms?

Many microorganisms live in and on the body without causing any harm. Some, like intestinal bacteria that help in the process of digestion, are actually beneficial. The body's immune system ignores these. Other microorganisms provoke an immediate immune response that attacks invading microorganisms.

White blood cells like this one help form part of the immune system.

The immune system acts as the body's private militia that mobilizes to protect its territory. Vomiting, diarrhea, coughing, sneezing, gaging, and tearing are some of the almost instant methods of clearing unwanted organisms from the body. Other immune tactics take longer.

For instance, when the skin is cut, bleeding begins. The flowing blood carries microorganisms away from the site of the injury. Platelets and blood clotting proteins move into the area to stem the blood flow. Other body chemicals react by migrating to the site, where they issue chemical commands that help the blood vessels accommodate for the injury. Visible damage repair begins as soon as bleeding stops. A scab begins forming to protect the healing skin.

Meanwhile, the immune system has already activated a variety of white blood cells (WBCs) that rush to the area to perform different duties. Neutrophils that engulf five to twenty-five bacterial cells arrive first. Other WBCs arrive at the scene in due time: eosinophils release enzymes to detoxify (neutralize) foreign proteins; basophils aid in controlling swelling; lymphocytes deliver a specific protein (antibody) that fights the protein (antigen) carried by the invaders; and finally, monocytes (enormous WBCs) swell to become macrophages that engulf up to one hundred bacterial cells. Depending on the severity of the injury, the immune system keeps pumping out these "reinforcements" until the infection "battle" ends.

CUTTING EDGE   SCIENCE

The immune response and microorganisms

The body's attack on invading microorganisms involves a cascade of events called an immune response. As soon as an infection is detected, the body rapidly produces extra white blood cells. The white blood cells (WBCs) mobilize to attack the microorganisms. Some specialized WBCs, called phagocytes, engulf the microorganisms and destroy them. Free-floating blood proteins called complements also react to the antigens of the invading cells by producing a reaction that coats the microorganisms with a substance that makes it easier for the phagocytes to target and destroy the invaders. In time, active immunity results: Some of the WBCs learn to "remember" the microorganism's antigen, and will react very quickly if it ever enters the body again. This is how someone becomes resistant to a disease.

CHAPTER 3

Treating Infectious Diseases

Four main ways to treat or prevent infectious diseases include medication, vaccination, hygienic practices, and natural remedies. Medications attack pathogens, such as antibiotics and antiviral drugs. Vaccines help the immune system produce antibodies to prevent disease. High standards of cleanliness prevent infections from occurring. In other words, listen to your mother—something as simple as proper handwashing goes a long way! Finally, many natural, or "folk remedies," use vitamins, minerals, herbs, and lifestyle changes to combat infectious diseases.

Antibiotics

Antibiotics attack bacteria. They have no effect on viruses, fungi, or parasites, and are therefore only useful in the treatment of bacterial infections. Although many people ask for antibiotics to treat a cold or the flu, no doctor should ever prescribe them for such conditions: Antibiotics cannot cure viral infections.

Antibiotics are taken by mouth as tablets or capsules. Some antibiotic creams and lotions are also available for treating skin infections. Someone with a severe infection may receive antibiotics through an intravenous drip system: The antibiotic solution travels through a tube straight into the patient's bloodstream. The amount

CUTTING EDGE MOMENTS

The discovery of the antibiotic penicillin

The discovery of penicillin came about by accident. In 1928, English scientist Alexander Fleming was studying the relationship between bacteria and diseases. He set up some culture dishes of bacteria in his lab and then went on vacation for a few days. When he returned, Fleming found that one of the dishes contained mold next to a clear patch where microbes had begun to grow but then died. Fleming grew some more of the mold and tested it by growing bacteria nearby. Fleming found that the mold produced a chemical that killed the microbes. The mold was *Penicillium notatum*, so Fleming decided to call the bacteria-killing chemical "penicillin."

of antibiotic being given is monitored and adjusted as the patient's condition worsens or improves.

Some antibiotics kill bacteria while others prevent them from multiplying, which allows the immune system to destroy the bacteria. Antibiotics that are effective against a wide range of bacteria are known as broad-spectrum antibiotics. These may be used when a patient is so seriously ill that doctors cannot waste time trying to identify the specific bacterium that is causing the infection. They are also used when a patient has an infection caused by several different types of bacteria. Other antibiotics, which are only effective against a limited range of bacteria, are known as narrow-spectrum antibiotics. They are useful when the specific bacterium responsible for the infection is known.

Alexander Fleming discovered penicillin in his laboratory.

CUTTING EDGE   SCIENCE

How do antibiotics kill microorganisms?

Some antibiotics damage the bacterial cell wall so that the bacteria slowly become leaky and die. Some antibiotics stop the bacteria from making new protein molecules, thus preventing them from functioning normally. Other antibiotics stop the bacteria from dividing properly. If bacteria cannot divide, they cannot reproduce, so any bacteria that die cannot be replaced.

Some of the first antibiotics used in the treatment of bacterial infections were a group of medicines known as sulfa drugs, developed in the 1930s. These drugs, created from chemical dyes, killed bacteria. Although sulfa drugs were important during World War II, they caused unpleasant side effects such as sickness and fever. The first antibiotic suitable for general use was penicillin. Commercial production of penicillin began during World War II, when it was used to treat injured soldiers. Soon after the war, it was made available to the general public. Scientists began to search for other antibiotic chemicals, and during the 1950s and 1960s, many new antibiotics were introduced.

Today, doctors have access to a large number of antibiotics. Different antibiotics are used to treat different types of bacterial infection. When antibiotics are prescribed, it is important that the patient finishes the course of treatment. If he or she stops taking the antibiotics too soon, some bacteria may survive and multiply; if this happens, the infection can break out again.

Antiviral drugs

Viruses are very small and will only grow inside other cells, so it has been more difficult to develop antiviral drugs than antibiotics. The first antiviral drugs were developed during the 1960s, but were only available for a few specific viruses. Since the 1980s, many more antiviral drugs have become available. This has been possible because modern techniques have helped scientists learn and understand more about viruses and how they behave.

Different antiviral drugs work in different ways. Some are specific to (effective against only) a single virus. For example, amantadine is effective against some strains of flu virus. It prevents virus particles from invading host cells. Zidovudine (AZT),which is effective against HIV, prevents the virus's genetic material from being copied. Other antiviral drugs, also specific to a single virus, work by preventing new virus particles from forming or by preventing the release of new virus particles from the host cell.

An alternative approach involves using medications to stimulate the body's own immune system to react to the virus particles. Some antiviral drugs, such as interferons, cause an immune reaction against a range of viruses. Interferons work by indirectly stimulating the body's immune system to attack the virus particles. Antibodies that stick to the virus particles serve as targets for the immune system to attack.

This micrograph shows crystals of ampicillin, an antibiotic used to treat infections such as bronchitis and typhoid.

Antifungal medicines

Fungal infections can be treated in a variety of ways. Most antifungal treatments work by damaging the fungal wall (*see page 22*), which kills the fungus. Antifungal creams, known as topical antifungals, can be rubbed on the surface of the infected area. Shampoos containing antifungal chemicals can be used to wash hair if the scalp is infected. Antifungal medicines to treat some fungal infections can be taken by mouth or given by injection.

CUTTING EDGE — SCIENCE

How do antifungal drugs work?

Because fungi are similar in many ways to animal cells, many potential treatments that would kill fungi also harm the patient's own cells. To avoid this, antifungal medicines must target the few differences that exist between animal and fungal cells. Some antifungal medicines work by attaching to specific chemicals in the fungal wall, making the wall leaky and thus killing the fungus. Other antifungal medicines work by preventing cell wall chemicals from being produced. Human cells do not contain cell wall chemicals, so the patient is not harmed.

Treating parasitic infections

Simple precautions can help avoid contracting parasitic infections in the first place. Different precautions apply for the various parasites found in the wide range of environments. Treatments for parasitic infections also differ according to the cause of the infection. Methods of prevention and treatment follow.

malaria Spray exposed body areas and clothes with insecticide; sleep under a mosquito net to avoid mosquito bites; take prophylactic medications before exposure to prevent an infection from developing.

schistosomiasis Avoid contact with infected water and rinse off thoroughly after contact with infected water.

tapeworms Cook all meat thoroughly.

Bark from this plant, *Cinchona succirubra*, was an original source of the antimalarial drug, quinine.

medicines One of the oldest medicines to combat parasitic infections is quinine, which has been used for centuries to treat malaria. Quinine was traditionally made from the powdered bark of a South American tree. Similar compounds are now synthesized (made in a laboratory) for commercial manufacture. Medicines that kill the parasite inside the body not only cure the infection in the person who takes the medicine, but also prevent the infection from being transmitted to others.

vaccines Vaccines contain a small amount of dead or weakened ("attenuated") infectious material. When introduced into the body, the vaccine primes the immune system to mount a defense against that organism in the future. If enough people are vaccinated against a disease, the disease will be brought under control and eventually die out.

insect control One way to contain the spread of a parasitic infection is to reduce the number of insects. Chemical insecticides, available as gels, sprays, and creams, help keep insects away. Smoke or vapors given off by certain substances can also control insects.

clean water Clean drinking water and improved sanitation can reduce the incidence (frequency) and spread of water-related infections, such as cholera or schistomosiasis.

Vaccines

Vaccines help fight against infectious diseases because they prevent
an infection from developing. A vaccine contains a small amount of
dead or weakened ("attenuated") microorganism that is injected into
a person's body. The vaccine does not cause a full-blown infection,
but it prompts the person's immune system to produce antibodies to
defend against the "foreign" material. If that microorganism enters
the body again, the immune system will instantly recognize the
invader and respond by destroying it before an infection can develop.
For some microorganisms, such as measles, a vaccination offers

A medical worker gives
this boy a tetanus booster
injection.

protection that lasts throughout a person's lifetime. For others, such as tetanus, the protection gradually becomes less effective and another injection, called a "booster," is necessary every few years.

Smallpox is a good example of the effectiveness of widespread vaccination. Before a vaccination was introduced, smallpox was a major worldwide killer. In 1967, the World Health Organization (WHO) introduced a worldwide vaccination program for smallpox. The last recorded case of smallpox occurred in 1977, and by 1980 WHO officially declared smallpox eradicated (wiped out). Today, only a few samples of smallpox bacteria remain. They are kept locked away in high-security, secret laboratories.

Vaccination also proved very successful against a crippling disease called poliomyelitis. Usually called polio, the diease often affected children. Polio causes muscle paralysis and, if it affects the chest muscles, can cause death by preventing the child from breathing. In 1952, more than 58,000 cases of polio occurred in the United States. After the introduction of a polio vaccine in 1954, the number of cases dropped rapidly. By the end of the decade, there were fewer than ten cases per year in the U.S. In 1994, the Americas were officially declared polio-free. Today, polio still occurs in India, Pakistan, and parts of Africa.

CUTTING EDGE   MOMENTS

The first vaccination

The first recorded vaccination occurred in 1796 by Edward Jenner, a doctor from Gloucestershire, England. Smallpox was an infectious disease that killed many people and left others badly scarred. People who lived in the countryside knew that dairymaids, who often caught a related but milder disease called cowpox, were much less likely to catch smallpox than others. Jenner thought that the cowpox might be giving them some protection against smallpox. To test his theory, he took some cowpox pus from the sores on a dairymaid's arm and scratched it into the arm of a healthy young boy. The boy caught cowpox and recovered. A few weeks later, Jenner repeated the process on the boy—but this time, Jenner used the deadly smallpox pus. The boy did not catch smallpox. Jenner's idea worked: by exposing people to cowpox, he could protect them against smallpox. His method became known as vaccination, after the latin word for cow, *vacca*.

Hygiene

Keeping ourselves, our clothes, our possessions, our food, and our surroundings hygienic can significantly reduce the likelihood of catching an infectious disease. For most people in developed countries, this is not too difficult. In some parts of the world where there is no clean water supply and inadequate sanitation, keeping their bodies, food, and living area clean proves extremely difficult.

Regular washing, showering, or bathing removes microorganisms from the skin's surface. Good personal hygiene in the bathroom is very important—many microorganisms leave the body in feces and are easily transferred to the hands. Most of these microorganisms can be removed by washing the hands thoroughly with soap. Inadequate hand washing can transfer microorganisms to other surfaces, such as towels and door handles—and from there to other people. Infections spread rapidly this way.

Immediately clean wounds with soap and clean water to minimize the risk of microorganisms entering the body via the damaged skin and causing an infection. Use one of the many modern products, such as antiseptic wipes, sprays, and creams that help keep wounds clean. A sterile dressing such as a band-aid covers the wound, keeps it clean, and provides a barrier to microorganisms until the skin can heal. Some over-the-counter (no prescription needed) salves also shorten the healing time.

CUTTING EDGE MOMENTS

Introduction of antiseptics

People did not begin to understand the link between lack of cleanliness and infectious disease until the late nineteenth century. At that time, many people who went to a hospital for treatment died of infections. Joseph Lister (1827–1912) was a Scottish surgeon who pioneered the introduction of effective hygiene in hospitals in the mid-1860s. The first chemical he used to combat infection was carbolic acid. Lister arranged for it to be sprayed in the operating rooms during surgeries, and he even used it directly on dressings for patients' wounds. The infection rates in Lister's hospital dropped rapidly. Slowly, other doctors adopted his methods. Dirty wounds that become infected are said to be "septic," so the chemicals that were developed to combat these infections became known as antiseptics.

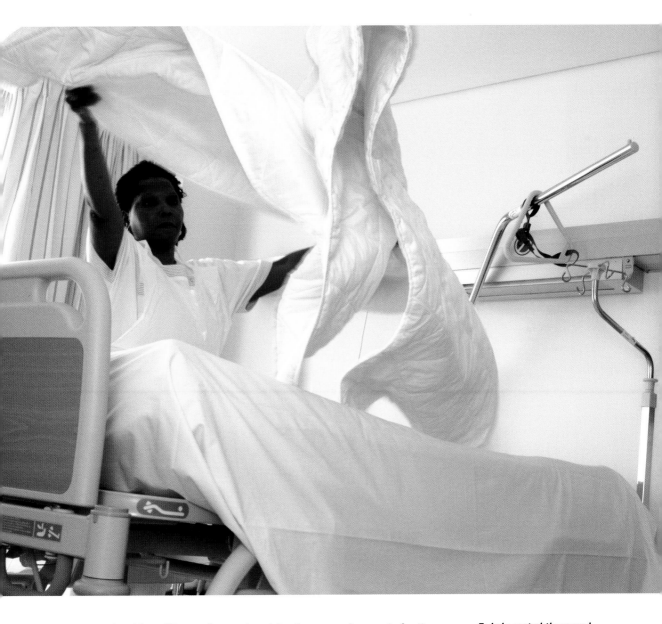

Proper food handling reduces the risk of contracting an infection. All utensils and working surfaces should be clean. Store, prepare, and cook foods at the correct temperatures. Containers that held raw foods must be washed before holding cooked foods.

Hygiene in hospitals prevents infections from spreading between patients. Frequent hand washing and the use of sterile instruments and dressings go a long way in disease prevention. A patient with a serious infection may be isolated (kept separated from contact with others) to prevent the infection from spreading.

To help control the spread of infection, each patient's linens are removed and sterilized in the laundry before being reused for another patient.

Natural remedies

Many people feel that there must be a better way to combat infectious diseases than waiting until an infection has developed and then using antibiotics or antiviral drugs to treat it. Preventing the infection from developing in the first place would be ideal. Vaccines can prevent many diseases, but people can also avoid contracting an infectious disease in other ways.

People can strengthen their body's immune system by eating a balanced diet. Some people also take herbs and vitamins. Natural herbs that supposedly promote a healthier immune system include echinacea, from the coneflower plant, and astragalus, from a type of pea plant. Vitamins, such as vitamins A, C, and E, and some minerals, such as zinc, magnesium, and selenium, have also been found to promote good health. (Astragalus is rich in selenium, which could be a reason for its effectiveness.)

Lifestyle improvements may also strengthen the immune system. People who reduce their intake of caffeine and alcohol, do not smoke or give up it up, exercise, and get adequate amounts of sleep, sunshine, and fresh air, boost their immune system.

A healthy digestive system contains millions of "good" bacteria that prevent harmful bacteria from entering the body. Without these good bacteria, we are much more likely to develop infections from harmful bacteria. Because antibiotics kill good bacteria as well as harmful ones, the use of antibiotics may deplete the natural

CUTTING EDGE   FACTS

Honey and wounds

People have always used "folk remedies" to find ways of healing their injuries. Many of the old treatments seem strange to us, and some have been proved to have no medical value. Scientists have discovered, however, that some ancient remedies really do work and have investigated the reasons for their effectiveness. For example, putting honey on wounds was once regarded as a standard remedy for helping the healing process. People believed that the honey helped clean and heal the wound. Although this may not sound like a very clean and hygienic approach, modern research has shown that there is a scientific basis for it: Honey contains a chemical called hydrogen peroxide that prevents infection.

bacteria found in our digestive system. We can replenish the good bacteria by adding a wider variety of natural foods to our diets. Yogurt contains healthy cultures of bacteria that aid disgestion, and the skins of many fruits and vegetables, such as apples and potatoes, also contain the so-called good bacteria.

Herbal tea can be made from dried eucalyptus leaves, which have antiseptic properties.

CHAPTER 4

Producing Antibiotics, Vaccines, and other Anti-infection Medications

Antibiotics, vaccines, and other anti-infection medications are commercially produced in large quantities. Every stage of the manufacturing process is carefully regulated and monitored to ensure the purity and safety of the medications. Advances in modern technology have improved production methods and have made significant contributions toward the research into new medications for combating infectious diseases.

Developing antibiotics

Since Alexander Fleming discovered the antibiotic properties of penicillin, many other scientists have been involved in the development of these medicines. Fleming himself was unable to

CUTTING EDGE   FACTS

Testing antibiotics

Before computers were widely used in science, all chemicals that had potential benefits as antibiotics were tested in laboratories. The chemical in question was mixed into a culture gel (a substance on which bacteria can grow), and small samples of different bacteria were placed on it. A chemical that prevented the growth of at least one of the bacteria samples showed value as an antibiotic. This method was slow and laborious. Now, computer modeling techniques can predict which chemicals will likely have antibiotic properties. Computer-controlled robots can handle large numbers of samples and test them more quickly and efficiently than human researchers could.

A researcher tests the sensitivity of bacteria to different antibiotics.

purify enough penicillin to test its use as a medicine. Two other scientists, Howard Florey and Ernst Chain, developed a method for testing its effectiveness, but penicillin was not produced on a commercial scale until after World War II.

Doctors often refer to "families of antibiotics." In other words, many antibiotics are closely related medications that share a common molecular core structure. U.S. scientist Lloyd H. Conover first discovered a relationship between antibiotics in 1955 while studying terramycin and aureomycin. He named their core structure "tetracycline." Other scientists soon discovered a different core for penicillin, which they called beta-lactam. Researchers often develop new antibiotics by slightly modifying these core structures.

The discovery of these cores made available a new range of antibiotics for use in the fight against infectious diseases. Some are extracted from fungi, bacteria, or plants—while others are synthesized in the laboratory.

Testing for safety

Scientists check the safety and efficacy (how it works and what side effects occur) of an antibiotic before commercial production begins. Side effects caused by drugs can range from minor problems, such as increased thirstiness, sweating, and headache, to much more serious complications, such as anemia, hearing loss, or permanent liver damage—and in extreme cases, even death.

Initially, researchers test cell cultures in the laboratory. Genetic material from the treated cells is tested for damage. If the antibiotic is found to have any adverse effects, it is abandoned and no further

CUTTING EDGE   DEBATES

Are animal tests necessary?

When your doctor prescribes a medicine, he or she should tell you about any side effects caused by that medication. Drug safety can only be achieved through exhaustive testing. Although many tests occur at the cell culture level, they do not provide information about how a drug may affect a body system or complete organism. Without this information, many people argue that it would be too risky to move straight to human tests. They say this risk justifies the need for testing new drugs on animals. Other people argue that it is wrong to use animals in medical research. The issue often sparks hot debates.

What do you think?

testing occurs. These initial cell culture tests also help researchers get an idea of how much is too much and what constitutes the correct amount of antibiotic used for treatment.

Animal testing of the antibiotic follows. Usually, small animals, such as mice, are subjected to huge quantities of the drug in question. Once researchers know the beneficial and adverse effects of an antibiotic, the drug testing (trials) are performed on larger animals, such as guinea pigs and rabbits.

Eventually, after an enormous number of animal tests have been completed, and the researchers are as confident as possible that they have determined what dosages and strengths to use, the new medication is tested on humans. The participants, or subjects, who are sometimes (but not always) paid for their participation, become part of a study called a clinical trial. Early clinical trials often involve only a small number of people. As researchers gather more information about the efficacy of a drug, further studies involving larger numbers of participants occur.

Most research divides participants into groups. Some subjects receive the study medication while others receive a placebo (a drug containing no active ingredients). The best design for research studies are "double-blind" trials. This means that neither the participants nor anyone on the research staff know who receives the trial medication and who receives the placebo. Subjects are

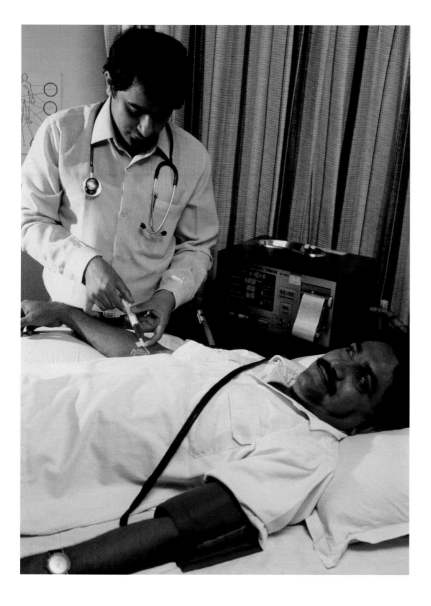

A technician takes a blood sample from a patient who is participating in a clinical drug trial.

identified only by code numbers. At the end of the trial, the information is decoded and researchers can see whether the study medication was more effective than the placebo. Researchers also break the study codes if the health of participants is endangered.

Production of medicines

Once researchers know that the new medicine is both effective and safe, large-scale production begins. The commercial production of antibiotics by fungi takes place in huge containers called fermentation tanks. These contain a liquid called growth medium, which provides all the nutrients the fungi need for growth.

Ideal conditions for fungi growth are necessary for the maximum amount of antibiotic production. To achieve this, researchers carefully monitor factors such as oxygen, temperature, acidity, and nutrient levels. Eventually, the antibiotic, which is a chemical by-product of the fungi, is extracted from the culture and purified.

Technicians who work with dangerous microbes use isolation and containment chambers like these to prevent infection and contamination.

Chemical synthesis of antibiotics also takes place in enormous quantities. There are often several stages in the process of converting chemicals into the final antibiotic.

Likewise, commercial production of vaccines occurs on a large scale. Researchers first isolate the pathogen that the vaccine must fight. Once the pathogen has been isolated, it is grown in large vats called biofermentation tanks. As with antibiotic production from fungi, the conditions within the vats must be perfect to ensure that optimal growth occurs. Because viruses cannot replicate on their own, the growth medium within the tanks must include microorganisms that can function as host cells.

Vaccines do not use a pathogen in its natural state because that would cause a full infection. Instead, the pathogen must be attenuated—changed, weakened, or killed—so that it prompts an immune reaction in the person receiving it without causing the disease. (In other words, the vaccinated person develops antibodies to the disease.) The attenuated virus is then mixed with other chemicals, and the resulting material forms the basis of the vaccine.

Each batch of vaccine is numbered and dated and then tested again to ensure that it meets strict safety criteria. It is tested for effectiveness against the intended pathogens. Other testing ensures that the vaccine is at the correct strength and is not contaminated. Once the vaccine meets all these requirements, it is approved for clinical use.

CUTTING EDGE MOMENTS

Growing viruses in the laboratory

When viruses were first observed in the 1930s, it was difficult to study them because there was no easy way to obtain enough virus material. The problem arose because viruses only grow inside other cells. A breakthrough came in 1948 when a team of U.S. scientists discovered that they could grow the mumps virus in fertilized chicken eggs. Virus material was injected into the eggs, and the virus multiplied inside the chick tissue. Using this method, scientists could grow large quantities of viruses, which allowed better studies of viruses and the development of vaccines. Although methods for producing and studying viruses have since improved, the breakthrough was a very important step in the science of virology.

Some vaccines offer protection against more than one disease. The MMR vaccine, for example, offers protection against measles, mumps, and rubella. To achieve this, material from each of the pathogens to which the vaccine offers protection must be mixed together. The finished vaccine is put into single-dose containers, such as syringes or bottles.

Large-scale, computer-controlled production of other anti-infection chemicals, such as antiseptics and antifungal medications, also occur. Pharmaceutical factories produce very large quantities of drugs at a time. Medications are mixed with other substances to stabilize the infection-fighting chemicals and to make the medicines suitable for use in whatever form they will be administered.

This doctor is prescribing a course of antibiotics to treat the patient's infection.

Medicines for treating infectious diseases are available in many different forms. Liquids, tablets, or capsules are taken orally (by mouth). Other liquid medications are given by injection, and still others are topical creams or salves rubbed onto the skin. Some are shampoos or mists. Doctors must stay up-to-date on information about the medicines available for treating different conditions.

Testing and monitoring

Government standards ensure that any medicines produced meet safety guidelines. Different governments have different sets of rules, but they all have the same goal: to protect the population by ensuring that all medicines produced are safe and will not knowingly cause harm to patients. Several government health agencies in the United States review the test results for antibiotics, vaccines, and all other new medications. If the drug meets the required standards, then the packaging, marketing, and distribution of the medicine begins.

Government agencies and drug companies themselves monitor approved medications (including those new to the market—as well as those that have been in use for years) for adverse side effects that may not have appeared during the testing period. Sometimes, even established medications cause major health problems, such as cancers or even deaths, after they have been used by thousands of people for a number of years. When that happens, the government or company may withdraw a medicine from the market for further testing, or its use may be banned completely.

CUTTING EDGE   FACTS

Overuse of antibiotics

Our reliance on antibiotics has contributed to the rise of microorganisms that become resistant to antibiotics (*see page 53*). In an attempt to combat this problem, doctors should only prescribe antibiotics when absolutely necessary. Patients can help fight this problem by not requesting antibiotics for minor infections. Also, patients should make sure to finish taking all of the medication prescribed for an illness—even after they begin to feel better and the symptoms seem to have disappeared. Maintaining good personal hygiene also helps prevent infections from occurring and spreading in the first place, which reduces the need for antibiotics.

CHAPTER 5

Overcoming Problems Fighting Infectious Diseases

Many problems arise in the fight against infectious disease. Some problems naturally occur, and others are caused by the actions of humans. While scientists are working to understand and reduce the natural incidence of infectious diseases around the world and to develop new cures and treatments, many human activities contribute to the spread of existing infectious diseases and the creation of new ones.

Mutation

Microorganism mutation poses a huge problem in fighting infectious diseases. Mutations can affect both the effectiveness of antibiotics and the development of vaccines. When a bacterium mutates, its molecular structure changes into a new strain that often renders an antibiotic useless for that infection. This has occurred repeatedly with a number of different bacteria and antibiotics. Scientists first reported the problem during the 1950s, when bacteria mutated so much that penicillin no longer worked to kill them. These bactera had become "resistant" to penicillin. Since then, more antibiotic-resistant bacterial strains have developed, making many of the older antibiotics useless. The best-known antibiotic-resistant bacterial

CUTTING EDGE   SCIENCE

What is mutation?
During cell division, all the genes of an organism are copied so that each new cell created receives a full set of genetic information. If errors occur during this copying process, the new cells will have different genetic information—and therefore slightly different characteristics—than the parent organism. These changes or errors are called mutations. Natural mutations, as well as those caused by external factors, such as exposure to radiation or chemicals, can occur during cell division. Some mutations help a cell survive, which increases the overall number of mutated cells.

strain is MRSA (methicillin-resistant *Staphylococcus aureus*), which causes serious problems with infection control in many hospitals.

It is becoming increasingly difficult to find antibiotics that can treat resistant strains of bacteria. Sometimes, it seems as if a bacteria becomes resistant to an antibiotic almost immediately. Some of the latest research reveals that certain bacteria actively participate in changing their own genomes by naturally producing proteins that cause the mutations. Doctors are trying to overcome this problem by prescribing antibiotics only when absolutely necessary. Also, they emphasize the importance of maintaining high standards of cleanliness to help reduce the spread of infectious diseases. The simple act of proper hand washing goes a long way in preventing the spread of diseases.

After the initial boom of antibiotic discoveries in the 1950s and 1960s, the rate of introduction of new antibiotics slowed considerably. The expensive process of developing and testing new antibiotics takes many years. Consequently, pharmaceutical companies (manufacturers of medical drugs) would rather invest their money in developing drugs that have more of an immediate financial reward, such as drugs for chronic (long term) diseases that affect large segments of the population.

This micrograph shows MRSA cells undergoing cell division. Many researchers call MSRA bacteria "superbugs" because no medications can stop them. Superbugs pose an enormous problem in the health care field. They can cause an infection to spread rapidly within the confines of a hospital.

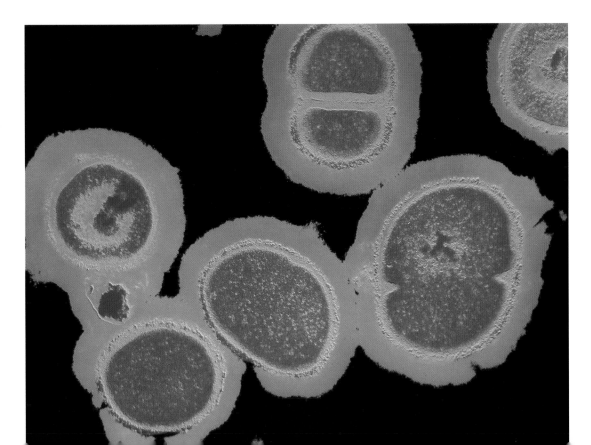

Viruses, such as influenza, also commonly mutate. Virus mutation makes vaccine development difficult. If a virus mutates into a new strain, the vaccine against the original may be ineffective against the new strain. Scientists must then work quickly to develop a vaccine that will counteract (fight) the new strain. If this new strain also mutates, another new vaccine will be needed. Vaccine researchers face a constant race to keep up with the mutations.

WHO researchers in the Ivory Coast, Africa, are part of the Ebola virus research team. Collecting specimens like this Colobus monkey skull may help them discover the origin of the virus.

Traditional lifestyles and beliefs

Scientists and medical workers around the world work hard to implement vaccination and treatment programs and raise people's awareness of the importance of hygiene and other health care issues. Many cultures, however, have deep-rooted beliefs and customs, and are sometimes suspicious and distrustful of new ideas. Theses attitudes can slow, prevent, or even reverse an improvement in the health of a community. For example, many local and religious groups in Nigeria, Africa, have vigorously opposed the polio vaccination program. Until recently, the disease was being brought under control there, but its incidence is now increasing because of cultural opposition to the procedure. The misinformation is also spreading from Nigeria to nearby areas where polio had previously been eradicated (wiped out).

Human activity

Some human activities have not only caused the appearance and spread of new infectious diseases, but also have made the infectious agent more virulent (stronger). As more humans travel widely and venture into remote wildlife habitats, they increase the incidence and frequency of exposure to infectious diseases endemic to local animal populations. Some diseases, such as Rift Valley fever (which originated in Kenya, Africa), Marburg fever, and Ebola virus (both of which originated in Uganda and the Democratic Republic of the Congo in Africa, respectively), were originally animal diseases that have mutated in a way that has caused them to infect humans.

Wars and natural disasters, such as famines and earthquakes, often result in movements of large numbers of people from their homes to refugee camps. Lack of adequate water and sanitation at these refugee camps can lead to outbreaks of infectious diseases.

Global warming and its associated climate changes will also alter the patterns of infection. For example, if average annual temperatures rise worldwide, pathogens once restricted to causing infections in hot climates will survive in other geographic areas.

CUTTING EDGE SCIENTISTS

Donald Hopkins

Donald Hopkins was born in 1941 and wanted to be a doctor for as long as he can remember. He studied at Morehouse College in Atlanta, Georgia, and as a student, visited Egypt. Following his experiences on that trip, he decided to specialize in studying and treating tropical diseases. Hopkins went on to study at the University of Chicago, Illinois, and at the Harvard School of Public Health in Boston, Massachusetts. He began work in 1967 with the Smallpox Eradication Program in Sierra Leone, Africa. In 1969, he returned to Harvard as Assistant Professor of Tropical Public Health. Three years later, he joined the U.S. Centers for Disease Control (CDC) in Atlanta, Georgia, eventually becoming its Deputy Director. Hopkins has worked with several global health organizations and has been a major driving force in the campaign to combat parasitic Guinea worm infections worldwide. Thanks to the efforts of Hopkins and his team, Guinea worm, which infected an estimated 3.5 million people in 1986, is now virtually eradicated, with only 11,500 cases reported in 2005.

CHAPTER 6

Current Developments

Many scientists around the world are working to find new ways to prevent and treat infectious diseases. Research laboratories are devoted to finding, synthesizing, and testing new chemicals. Computer modeling predicts useful chemical structures and patterns of disease spread and control. Other research focuses on improving production methods.

Microbiologists work to increase their understanding of microorganisms and devise new methods to combat them. Immunologists investigate the human immune system in order to increase their knowledge of how the body responds to infections. Geneticists—scientists who study the genetic material (genomes) of humans and other organisms—examine the genomes of many animals as they search for new anti-infection techniques.

Scientists are also looking outside the laboratory for new ways to fight infectious disease. Some study traditional remedies used by native peoples, while others investigate antibiotic chemicals found in animals (*see pages 58–59*).

New antibiotics

Chemists and computer specialists work together to develop new antibiotic chemicals. They use existing antibiotics as a starting point and employ computers to help predict the effects of tiny changes in the structures of the drugs. Chemists then narrow their research to include only those chemicals pinpointed by the computers as being potentially useful.

Production improvements

Research conducted in space yielded information that may help produce antibiotics derived from fungi. Experiments conducted aboard the space shuttle *STS-80* in 1996 revealed that microorganisms grow more quickly in zero-gravity conditions than on Earth. For example, the bacteria *Streptomyces plicatus* grew more quickly in space and produced the antibiotic actinomycin D at a faster rate than on Earth. Scientists are investigating why this happens and whether or not it will enable them to improve existing methods of producing antibiotics from fungi.

The immune system

The immune system relies on complex patterns of interactions between cells (*see page 31*). Researchers hope to garner more details regarding which cells are involved and how they affect each other. Scientists believe this information will help in developing medicines that will boost the immune system response to infections.

The Human Genome Project, completed in 2003, which mapped the full sequence of human genes, may increase our understanding of the immune system. Scientists plan to study the genome to identify and study the genes that trigger immune responses.

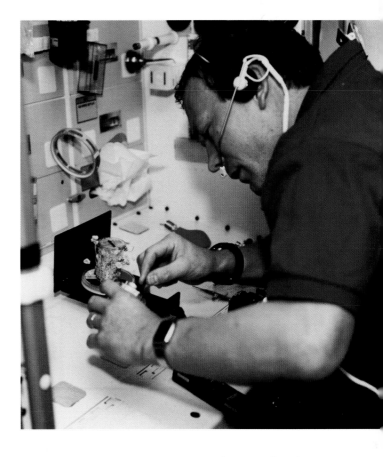

Experiments conducted aboard the *International Space Station* or one of the U.S. space shuttle missions provide excellent opportunities for investigating how organisms react to zero-gravity conditions.

CUTTING EDGE FACTS

Using mathematics and statistics

Epidemiologists—people who study the causes and spread of diseases—use computer modeling to predict the effects of different methods of controlling diseases. Such information could play an important role in the effective planning and monitoring of a worldwide response if a pandemic infection breaks out. A century and a half after the pioneering work of John Snow, scientists still work hard at understanding, preventing, and controlling diseases.

Plasmids

Many bacteria contain tiny rings of genetic material called plasmids, which are separate from the genetic material that makes up the bacterial chromosome. Geneticists have found that some plasmids seem to be involved in the development of antibiotic resistance. A bacterial cell can contain one or many plasmids, which can transfer from one bacterial cell to another, making each cell they enter resistant. Other plasmids can "turn off" the resistance, making the bacteria sensitive to antibiotics again. Some scientists think that it may be possible to use plasmids to overcome antibiotic resistance.

Studying traditional remedies

The world's rain forests contain a vast number of species of plants and animals, many of which are still unknown. Native peoples have long used rain forest materials in traditional remedies. For example, the plant called snakeroot, used by the Seneca Nation of Native Americans, has been found to have antibiotic and antifungal properties. Researchers often gather information from native peoples and visit diverse environments to collect plant samples. In the laboratory, plant samples are analyzed and the chemicals they contain are tested. Investigators believe that new medicines, such as antibiotics, may be discovered from this research.

CUTTING EDGE — SCIENCE

Deadly saliva

The Komodo dragon, which is indigenous (native to) Indonesia, is the largest species of lizard in the world. These carnivores often kill their prey in a single attack. Just one bite by a Komodo dragon is fatal because of its deadly saliva—it contains a range of bacteria that infects and kills prey. Scientists wondered why, if the saliva contains so many lethal bacteria, it does not harm the Komodo dragon itself. Scientists are analyzing samples of Komodo dragon saliva and blood to find out whether they contain antibiotics or other chemicals that may protect the dragons. This information may lead to the discovery of new antibiotics that can be used to treat humans. Geneticists are also studying the dragon's genome to see whether it is genetically resistant to bacteria; if so, that knowledge may help in the development of a genetic therapy for infectious disease in humans.

The skin of this Amazonian tree frog produces chemicals that have antibiotic properties.

Learning from plants and animals

Another area of disease research focuses on the defense mechanisms used by different species of animal. Scientists hope that this will lead to the development of new modes of treatment and protection. For example, scientists studying capuchin monkeys from South America discovered that the monkeys rub millipedes into their skin at the time of year when insect bites are most common. Analysis of the chemicals in the millipedes revealed that their bodies contain an insect-repellent chemical.

Scientists also study plant and animal species that appear to have a natural resistance to infection. They have found that many species produce antibiotic chemicals in their bodies. The first such discovery occurred in 1986, when the skin of the African clawed frog native to southern Africa was found to contain an antibiotic called magainin. Magainin is active against a wide range of pathogens, including bacteria, protozoa, and fungi. Since then, more antibiotic chemicals have been found in crocodile blood, seaweeds, pigs' guts, and silk moths. Each of these chemicals may prove invaluable in the development of future generations of antibiotics.

Glossary

antibiotic A chemical used to control bacterial infection.

antibody A chemical produced by white blood cells in response to an antigen.

antiseptic A chemical that kills microorganisms.

antiviral Capable of destroying or inactivating viruses.

attenuate To produce a change in the natural potency of a virus that makes it incapable of causing disease.

bacteria A type of microorganism that has a cell wall, a nucleus, its own DNA, and is capable of reproducing itself.

booster shot A repeated dose of a vaccine to maintain a person's level of immunity.

by-product A secondary substance produced in addition to the main product.

carnivores Animals that eat other animals.

cell The smallest unit of a living organism.

colony A group of bacteria.

contraceptive Something used or taken to prevent a pregnancy.

culture The growing of biological material in the laboratory, or the biological material itself.

cytoplasm The parts of a plant or animal cell outside the nucleus.

efficacy The effectiveness and safety of a drug.

endemic Occurs naturally in a particular place.

enzyme A protein that speeds up a chemical reaction that is essential to life.

epidemic An outbreak of infectious disease affecting many people.

epidemiology The study of the spread and causes of diseases.

eradicated Destroyed or wiped out so that it can never recur.

famine A severe shortage of food resulting in widespread hunger.

ferment To use micoorganisms, such as yeasts, to break down a substance into simpler ones.

fission Splitting into two.

flagellae Slender, threadlike structures on many microorganisms, used as a means of locomotion.

fruiting bodies A part of certain fungi from which spores are released.

fungi A microorganism that is neither plant nor animal and has hyphae instead of normal cells.

genetic Having to do with passing hereditary information from one generation to the next.

host cell A cell occupied by a virus or its genetic material in order for the virus to reproduce.

Human Genome Project The research project that mapped the complete set of human genes.

hygienic Clean.

hypodermic Under the skin.

immune system The body's natural defense mechanism to protect itself from harm.

incidence Frequency.

infectious Can spread from person to person.

intravenous Into a vein.

isolated Kept away from; also, occurring only rarely and unlikely to recur.

larva An early stage in the life cycle of some organisms.

lethal Causing or able to cause death.

localized infection An infection that affects only a small area of the body.

lymphocyte A type of white blood cell.

microorganism A living organism that is too small to be seen with the naked eye.

microscope An instrument that magnifies objects too small to see with the naked eye.

nucleus The part of a cell that contains the genetic information.

nutrients Substances that provide nourishment, such as the ingredients in food, that keep a body healthy and help it grow.

oral Relating to the mouth.

organ A tissue or tissues that perform a single specific bodily function or related functions.

pandemic A disease outbreak affecting a large number of people over a wide geographic area.

parasite An organism that gets its nourishment from another organism (a host), which it harms.

pathogen An organism that causes disease.

placebo An inactive chemical used in clinical trials as a "control" drug.

plasmid A small, circular portion of DNA, found in bacterial cells.

prophylactic A biological or mechanical method for preventing disease.

proteins An important group of natural substances that help form skin, hair, and muscle, and that also control processes inside cells.

protozoa A single-celled organism.

quarantine To keep away from others in order to prevent the spread of infection.

resistant Unaffected; for example, the disease does not develop even after exposure to it.

respiration (as in cellular respiration) The process by which a cell breaks down glucose (a type of sugar) in order to obtain energy.

sanitation Methods for removing waste.

septic Dirty.

side effects Usually undesirable secondary effects of a drug or other form of medical treatment.

spores Small, usually one-celled, reproductive structures produced by fungi that are capable of developing into a new individual.

synthetic Not occurring naturally; human-made.

system Organs and tissues that work together to carry out a single function or related functions.

tissue Cells of one type organized to perform a single function.

toxin A poison; a natural chemical produced by some microorganisms that causes illnesses.

vaccine A substance used to produce immunity to a disease.

vector An organism, such as a mosquito, that transmits disease-causing microorganisms from infected individuals to people, or from infected animals to humans.

virus A type of microorganism that often causes diseases and can only reproduce inside a host cell.

Further Information

BOOKS

Bédoyère, Guy de la. *The Discovery of Penicillin.* Milestones In Modern Science (series). World Almanac® Library (2006).

Bédoyère, Guy de la. *The First Polio Vaccine.* Milestones In Modern Science (series). World Almanac® Library (2006).

Morgan, Sally. *Fight Against Disease.* Science at the Edge (series). Heinemann Library (2003).

Parker, Steve. *Microlife that Makes Us Ill.* Amazing World of Microlife (series). Raintree (2006).

Parker, Steve. *Defend Yourself: The Immune System.* Body Talk (series). Raintree (2006).

Routh, Kristina. *AIDS*: 21st Century Issues (series). World Almanac® Library (2005).

Snedden, Robert. *Fighting Infectious Disease.* Microlife (series). Heinemann Library (2000).

Walker, Pam, and Elaine Wood. *The Immune System.* Understanding the Human Body (series). Lucent (2002).

WEB SITES

www.bacteriamuseum.org
Take a virtual tour of the museum of bacteria.

www.kidshealth.org/Search01.jsp
Follow the links for information about diseases that may affect young people.

www.microbeworld.org
Explore a wealth of information and activities regarding microorganisms and meet some of the scientists who specialize in studying them.

www.tulane.edu/ ~ dmsander/WWW/ Video/pneumo.mov
Watch as bacteria multiply. (Quicktime required.)

www.ucmp.berkeley.edu/bacteria /bacteria.html
Discover the fossil history, ecology, and life cycles of bacteria.

Index

63

Index (continued)